THE WIT AND WISDOM
OF
ADLAI STEVENSON

The Wit and Wisdom

of

ADLAI STEVENSON

Compiled by

Edward Hanna
Henry Hicks
Ted Koppel

Hawthorn Books, Inc., *Publishers*
New York and London

First Edition, August, 1965

Acknowledgments

Our many thanks are extended to Wide World Photos for permission to use photographs. Permission to reprint passages in the text is also gratefully acknowledged.

Passages from the record album "The Wit of JFK" (VDM—101) are included through the permission of RCA Victor.

Passages from the book *Major Campaign Speeches of Adlai E. Stevenson,* copyright © 1953, are included here with the kind permission of Random House.

The photograph on page 95 is reproduced through the courtesy of Cornell Capa/Magnum.

We are also grateful to Tom O'Brien, Vice-President for Radio News, American Broadcasting Company, for his co-operation; to John MacVane and Mal Goode, ABC News correspondents at the United Nations, for their assistance; to Catharine Lynch, ABC Librarian, for locating for us much valuable material; and to Mary White and Elizabeth Levy, for outstanding research endeavor.

H-9387

To the memory of the man who wrote this book

THE WIT AND WISDOM
OF
ADLAI STEVENSON

Eggheads, unite! You have nothing to lose but your yolks.

———◆———

The costliest blunders have been made by dictators who did not quite understand the working of real democracy and who mistook diversity for disunity.

San Francisco, California
September 9, 1952

The struggle between faith and fear will decide the destiny of our nation.

Los Angeles, California
September 11, 1952

The contest with tyranny is not a hundred-yard dash —it is a test of endurance.

San Francisco, California
September 9, 1952

We doubt whether any nation has so absolute a grip on absolute truth that it is entitled to impose its idea of what is right on others.

The New York Times Magazine
November 4, 1962

The challenge to all of us is to prove that a free society can remain free, humane, and creative, even when it is under heavy and ruthless fire; that it can combat poverty, injustice, and intolerance in its own midst, even while resisting a monstrous foreign despotism; and that it can give men a glimpse of serenity and hope, even while calling on them for sacrifice.

To the State Committee of the Liberal Party
New York, New York
August 28, 1952

We dare not just look back to great yesterdays. We must look forward to great tomorrows.

Welcoming address
Democratic National Convention
Chicago, Illinois
July 21, 1952

When we have come so far we know we can go farther.

Labor Day rally, Cadillac Square
Detroit, Michigan
September 1, 1952

A hungry man is not a free man.

Kasson, Minnesota
September 6, 1952

As citizens of this democracy you are the rulers and the ruled. The law-givers and the law-abiding, the beginning and the end.

Chicago, Illinois
September 29, 1952

Government (in a democracy) cannot be stronger or more tough-minded than its people. It cannot be more inflexibly committed to the task than they. It cannot be wiser than the people.

Chicago, Illinois
September 29, 1952

Slavery has ended but some of the evils of indignity and inequality it fostered still live on in our society. That is the dilemma of our day. Until we cope with it, we shall not cope with our new and irrevocable environment . . . and environment we ignore at our peril. We will get through the vast social revolution of our day on one condition only . . . that we face it with information and reason and not ignorance and fear.

Commencement address
Colby College
Waterville, Maine
June 7, 1964

Referring to racial violence:

Civil wrongs don't make civil rights . . . civil wrongs probably only beget civil wrongs.

"Issues and Answers" (ABC)
April 19, 1964

[9]

I utterly reject the argument that we ought to grant all men their rights just because if we do not we shall give Soviet Russia a propaganda weapon. This concept is itself tainted with Communist wiliness. It insultingly implies that were it not for the Communists we would not do what is right. The answer to this argument is that we must do what is right for right's sake alone.

Richmond, Virginia
September 21, 1952

I yield to no man, if I may borrow that majestic parliamentary phrase, in my belief in the principle of free debate, inside or outside the halls of Congress. The sound of tireless voices is the price we pay for the right to hear the music of our own opinions. But there is also a moment at which democracy must prove its capacity to act. Every man has a right to be heard; but no man has the right to strangle democracy with a single set of vocal cords.

New York, New York
August 28, 1952

The natural government of man is servitude, tyranny. It is only by intense thought, by great effort, by burning idealism and unlimited sacrifice that freedom has prevailed. And the efforts which were first necessary to create it are fully as necessary to sustain it in our own day.

Washington, D.C.
January, 1959

Government is like a pump, and what it pumps up is just what we are, a fair sample of the intellect, the ethics, and the morals of the people, no better, no worse.

Los Angeles, California
September 11, 1952

Corruption in public office is treason.
Colorado Volunteers for Stevenson Dinner
Denver, Colorado
September 5, 1952

My opponents say that the threat to our liberty comes from within. I say that the threat comes from without—and I offer the fate of the enslaved peoples of the world as my evidence.
Louisville, Kentucky
September 27, 1952

Our objectives are not for the timid. They are not for those who look backward, who are satisfied with things as they are, who think that this great nation can ever sleep or ever stand still.
Acceptance speech
Democratic National Convention
Chicago, Illinois
August 17, 1956

I wish the world could better know this country for what it really is—not just a greedy economic giant crouching fearfully behind its walls—not just a panoplied warrior nervously fingering his weapons—and not a sordid civil war between the officers of our government—but as *this*—as a people who gather together in thousands to give a people's government its essential vitality.
Hollywood Bowl
Hollywood, California
October 9, 1954

The government must be the trustee for the little man, because no one else will be. The powerful can usually help themselves—and frequently do!

Democratic rally
Duluth, Minnesota
October 29, 1955

Government by the consent of the governed is the most difficult system of all because it depends for its success and viability on the good judgments and wise decisions of so many of us.

Major Campaign Speeches of Adlai E. Stevenson
Random House, 1953

There are only three rules of sound administration: pick good men, tell them not to cut any corners, and back them to the limit.

Joseph Alsop in the Saturday Evening Post
Quoting Adlai Stevenson
June 28, 1952

Since the beginning of time, governments have been mainly engaged in kicking people around. The astonishing achievement of modern times in the Western world is the idea that the citizen should do the kicking.

What I Think
By Adlai E. Stevenson
Harper and Row, 1955

There are four reasons why a man leaves government service—family, finances, and frustration. . . .

"Issues and Answers" (ABC)
April 19, 1964

[13]

It is not enough to affirm our loyalty to existing laws and institutions . . . they must be changed for the better. We must be patriotic in the sense of being disinterested when healthy change imposes penalties upon us; magnanimous in recognizing that large national groups have suffered from injustice and have a right to expect reform; and public-spirited in supporting new ideas and new policies.

Does anyone seriously think that a real traitor will hesitate to sign a loyalty oath? Of course not. Really dangerous subversives will be caught by careful, constant, professional investigation, not by pieces of paper.

Veto of State Senate Bill 102
An antisubversive measure
Springfield, Illinois
June 27, 1951

The whole notion of loyalty inquisitions is a natural characteristic of the police state, not of democracy . . .

Veto of State Senate Bill 102
An antisubversive measure
Springfield, Illinois
June 27, 1951

We must fight traitors with laws. We already have the laws. We must fight falsehood and evil ideas with truth and better ideas. We have them in plenty. We must not confuse the two. Laws infringing our rights and intimidating un-

offending persons without enlarging our security will neither catch subversives nor win converts to our better ideas.

Acceptance speech
Democratic National Convention
Chicago, Illinois
July 26, 1952

Stevenson included this sentence in a message vetoing an "antisubversive" bill passed by the Illinois legislature:

To question even by implication the loyalty and devotion of a large group of citizens is to create an atmosphere of suspicion and distrust which is neither justified, healthy, nor consistent with our traditions.

Springfield, Illinois
June 27, 1951

Idealism in modern times has not always been fashionable. Unless something be justified by hard-headed self-interest it is said to have no chance. But let us remember that kindness and idealism may be practical too—and practical or not, they stand well in the eyes of God.

Great Issues Lecture
University of Texas
September 28, 1955

I think one of the greatest compliments that ever befell me was by the man who introduced me as a "practical idealist"—sort of a hard-boiled egghead, he said.

To Convention of Textile Workers Union of America
Chicago, Illinois
June 1, 1960

Humility and modesty, not pride or arrogance, must be the badges of our greatness.

Great Issues Lecture
University of Texas
September 28, 1955

The anatomy of patriotism is complex. But surely intolerance and public irresponsibility cannot be cloaked in the shining armor of rectitude and of righteousness. Nor can the denial of the right to hold ideas that are different— the freedom of man to think as he pleases. To strike freedom of the mind with the fist of patriotism is an old and ugly subtlety.

To the American Legion
Madison Square Garden
New York, New York
August 27, 1952

When an American says that he loves his country, he means not only that he loves the New England hills, the prairies glistening in the sun, the wide and rising plains, the great mountains, and the sea. He means that he loves an inner air, an inner light in which freedom lives and in which a man can draw the breath of self-respect.

New York, New York
August 27, 1952

My definition of a free society is a society where it is safe to be unpopular.

Detroit, Michigan
October 7, 1952

What do we mean by patriotism in the context of our times? . . . a patriotism that puts country ahead of self; a patriotism which is not short, frenzied outbursts of emotion, but the tranquil and steady dedication of a lifetime. These are words that are easy to utter, but this is a mighty assignment. For it is often easier to fight for principles than to live up to them.

To the American Legion
Madison Square Garden
New York, New York
August 27, 1952

Patriotism is not the fear of something; it is the love of something . . . Patriotism with us is not hatred of Russia; it is love of this republic; it is love of the ideal of liberty of man and of mind in which this republic was born and to which it is dedicated.

To the American Legion
Madison Square Garden
New York, New York
August 27, 1952

We must be on our guard against the danger to our own people, as well to our friends, of confusing pronouncements with reality and proclamations with policy. For these are the ingredients of extremist opinion. And in these days when moderation and reason are so often equated with appeasement or even disloyalty, we must be careful lest unreason and extremism not only frighten and alienate our friends and fan the flames of neutralism in the world but also mislead the American people.

Godkin Lectures
Harvard University
March, 1954

[18]

We will win the contest of ideas that afflicts the world not by suppressing these rights but by their triumph. We must not burn down the house to kill the rats.

Veto of State Senate Bill 102
An antisubversive measure
Springfield, Illinois
June 27, 1951

The following three quotes are from a speech before the Democratic National Committee's Southern Conference Dinner, closely following Senator Joseph McCarthy's attack on the Democratic Administration as "twenty years of treason":

Extremism produces extremism, lies beget lies . . .

Those who live by the sword of slander, also may perish by it . . .

When demagoguery and deceit become a national political movement, we Americans are in trouble, not just Democrats, but all of us.

Miami Beach, Florida
March 7, 1954

Those who corrupt the public mind are just as evil as those who steal from the public purse.

Albuquerque, New Mexico
September 12, 1952

To Defense Secretary Charles Wilson's "What's good for General Motors is good for the country" statement, Stevenson replied:

There's always the tendency to mistake the particular interest for the general interest. To suppose, in the immortal thought recently uttered before a committee of Congress, that what is good for General Motors is good for the country. There is always the possibility that the successor of the New Deal will turn out, after the fine words have faded away, to be the Big Deal, while the New Dealers have all left Washington to make way for the Car Dealers. I hasten to say that I, for one, do not believe the story that the general welfare has become a subsidiary of General Motors.

Jefferson Day Dinner
New York, New York
February 14, 1953

[Statesmanship] consists sometimes not so much in knowing what to do ultimately as in what to do now.

Los Angeles, California
September 12, 1952

Your public servants serve you right; indeed, often they serve you better than your apathy and indifference deserve.

Los Angeles, California
September 11, 1952

No matter how lofty you are in your department, the responsibility for what your lowliest assistant is doing is yours.

Springfield, Illinois
October 21, 1952

Centralization of governmental functions at higher and higher levels should be avoided. The states should not abdicate their responsibilities.

Springfield, Illinois
October 21, 1952

While I want you to sweep me down there [Washington], don't sweep any more government jurisdiction down there.

Governor's Day
Illinois State Fair
Springfield, Illinois
August 14, 1952

We believe that it is better to discuss a question even without settling it, than to settle a question without discussing it. And to conduct this discussion the party system has sprung up, based upon the premise that no one political organization has a monopoly on truth and reason.

What I Think
By Adlai E. Stevenson
Harper and Row, 1955

It seems to me sad that "politics" and "politician" are so often epithets and words of disrespect and contempt, and not without justification, in the land of Jefferson and in a government by the governed.

Major Campaign Speeches of Adlai E. Stevenson
Random House, 1953

It is the urgent duty of a political leader to lead, to touch if he can the potentials of reason, decency, and humanism in man, and not only the strivings that are easier to mobilize.

Major Campaign Speeches of Adlai E. Stevenson
Random House, 1953

I discovered that in a political job there are usually two ways to do things: the politically expedient way or the right way. Sometimes they do not coincide but in the long run the right way is the best politics.

Major Campaign Speeches of Adlai E. Stevenson
Random House, 1953

"Thou shalt not bear false witness" is still the law of God and man, I hope. And "Thou shalt not be afraid to bear true witness" is, I think, a good rule for all of us, including timid politicians.

Major Campaign Speeches of Adlai E. Stevenson
Random House, 1953

Self-criticism is the secret weapon of democracy, and candor and confession are good for the political soul.

Welcoming address
Democratic National Convention
Chicago, Illinois
July 21, 1952

I think self-examination and criticism are the great and not-so-secret weapons of democracy . . . as Marse Henry Watterson said, "Things have come to a pretty pass when a man can't cudgel his own jackass."

Major Campaign Speeches of Adlai E. Stevenson
Random House, 1953

The best government is in fact the best politics and will pay off in public confidence and votes manyfold what it loses in patronage, profit, and political organization.

Major Campaign Speeches of Adlai E. Stevenson
Random House, 1953

In 1952, prior to the Democratic nomination, Stevenson asked the Illinois delegation not to enter his name as a candidate. He was most sincere about this. When asked what he would do if he were nominated, he replied:

I think I'd shoot myself.

When he did indeed receive the nomination in 1952, he said this to the convention:

I have asked the merciful Father, the Father of us all, to let this cup pass from me. But from such dread responsibility one does not shrink in fear, in self-interest, or in false humility. . . . That my heart has been troubled, that I have not sought this nomination, that I could not seek it in good conscience, that I would not seek it in honest self-appraisal is not to say that I value it the less. Rather it is that I revere the office of the Presidency of the United States.

Acceptance speech
Democratic National Convention
Chicago, Illinois
July 26, 1952

I don't feel like a gift from Providence, and I really don't believe I am. I feel very much like a corn-fed Illinois lawyer who had gotten into the big time unintentionally.

Denver, Colorado
September 6, 1952

In my very brief political career I've sometimes wondered if I had any friends left. And then they suddenly nominated me for President, and I wondered if I hadn't too many friends.

To the State Committee of the Liberal Party
New York, New York
August 28, 1952

I ask of you all you have; I will give to you all I have.

Acceptance speech
Democratic National Convention
Chicago, Illinois
July 26, 1952

Forthright discussion of the real public questions is neither beneath the dignity of political candidates nor above the intelligence of the American people.

Los Angeles, California
September 11, 1952

You may properly ask of me, how I would conduct myself in this campaign. Well, to that I can only reply that I have been your leader before, and you must be familiar by this time with the merchandise. Now it's aged a bit, but it hasn't changed; and in spite of all the stories I hear about the new Stevenson who is shortly to be unveiled, indeed I'm cheered by the unanimity of disagreement about what this new model will be, and I suggest that maybe there are no surprises, and it will be the same old model.

Acceptance speech
Democratic National Convention
Chicago, Illinois
August 17, 1956

I promise no easy solutions, no relief from burdens and anxieties, for to do this would be not only dishonest, it would be to attack the foundations of our greatness. I can offer something infinitely better: an opportunity to work and sacrifice that freedom may flourish.

Louisville, Kentucky
September 27, 1952

I don't believe irresponsible promises are good politics. Promise-peddling and double-talk may be expedient and catch some votes from the unwary and innocent, but promises also have a way of coming home to roost.

Peru, Illinois
1948

In the long run, I believe you win by doing what you think is right, and explaining your reasons sensibly and straightforwardly to the voters.

Joseph Alsop in the Saturday Evening Post
Quoting Adlai Stevenson
June 28, 1952

I don't know yet whether one can win an election with hard, distasteful truths, but this is the only way I want to win it.

Radio broadcast to the Armed Forces overseas
August 30, 1952

I shall not try to win your vote by an "all this and heaven too" campaign.

Radio broadcast to the Armed Forces overseas
August 30, 1952

More important than winning the election is governing the nation. That is the test of a political party—the acid, final test.

Acceptance speech
Democratic National Convention
Chicago, Illinois
July 26, 1952

I believe that in ninety-nine cases out of a hundred, the American people will make the right decision—if and when they are in possession of the essential facts about any given issues.

Fairfield, Illinois
June, 1950

Some things are more precious than votes.

Hamtramck, Michigan
September 1, 1952

They say I am a "captive" of the city bosses, then of the CIO, and then of the Dixiecrats . . . and then of Wall Street, and then of an organization called ADA. Next week I'll probably read in the papers that I am the captive of a girl named Ada. I have not met her yet. I had no idea I was so popular, and I hope I can bear this multiple courtship and captivity with becoming modesty.

Springfield, Illinois
August 14, 1952

To catch some votes, or for fear of losing some, many things are done which seem to me hard to distinguish from outright bribery.

Los Angeles, California
September 11, 1952

Let's talk sense to the American people. Let's tell them the truth, that there are no gains without pains.

Acceptance speech
Democratic National Convention
Chicago, Illinois
July 26, 1952

I'm not an old experienced hand at politics. But I am now seasoned enough to have learned that the hardest thing about any political campaign is how to win without proving that you are unworthy of winning.

Fresno, California
October 11, 1956

A campaign addressed not to men's minds and to their best instincts, but to their passions, emotions and prejudices, is unworthy at best. Now, with the fate of the nation at stake, it is unbearable.

Chicago, Illinois
September 6, 1952

On the rigors of campaigning, he observed:

You must write at every chance, think if possible, read mail and newspapers, talk on the telephone, talk to everybody . . . and ride through city after city on the back of an open car, smiling until your mouth is dehydrated by the wind, waving until the blood runs out of your arms . . . bounce gaily, confidently, masterfully into great howling halls, shaved and all made up for television with the right color shirt and tie—I always forgot—and a manuscript so defaced with chicken tracks and last-minute jottings that

[30]

you couldn't follow it, even if the spotlights weren't blinding and even if the still photographers didn't shoot you in the eye every time you looked at them.

Major Campaign Speeches of Adlai E. Stevenson
Random House, 1953

There are only two points to bear in mind. The first is that political organizations are necessary and useful parts of our political system. The second is that good government is better politics than all the jobs in Christendom.

Joseph Alsop in the Saturday Evening Post
Quoting Adlai Stevenson
June 28, 1952

The true function of a political leader in a democracy is not to impose his will upon the people but to aid them in making proper choices . . . the political leader only proposes, but the people dispose.

To the Abraham Lincoln Association
Springfield, Illinois
February 12, 1952

If he [the candidate] purported to know the right answer to everything, he would be either a knave or a fool. If he even had an answer to everything, he would probably be just a fool. If he had no emphatic views at all, he would probably be just as unworthy, and if he were evasive, he would probably be either cunning or a political coward, of which we have altogether too many. And, finally, if he should arrive at election time with almost everybody satisfied, then you should, by all means, vote against him as the most dangerous charlatan of them all.

Los Angeles, California
September 11, 1952

[32]

This idea that you can merchandise candidates for high office like breakfast cereal—that you can gather votes like box tops—is, I think, the ultimate indignity to the democratic process.

Acceptance speech
Democratic National Convention
Chicago, Illinois
August 17, 1956

The Republicans have a "me too" candidate running on a "yes but" platform, advised by a "has been" staff.

Fort Dodge, Iowa
October 5, 1952

The real question is whether a platform represents the clicking of a ghost's typewriter, if I may put it that way, or the beating of a human heart.

To the State Committee of the Liberal Party
New York, New York
August 28, 1952

Platforms are supposed to be solemn, sincere public declarations of party principles and intentions. In fact, they are more often, in our times, disingenuous appeals to as many interests as possible to catch as many votes as possible. The people know this, by and large, and the result has been, it seems to me, that platforms per se not only attract fewer and fewer votes, but have come to mean less and less to more and more, candidates included.

Major Campaign Speeches of Adlai E. Stevenson
Random House, 1953

In politics there is neither gratitude nor mercy.

Joseph Alsop in the Saturday Evening Post
Quoting Adlai Stevenson
June 28, 1952

Senator Taft is the greatest living authority on what General Eisenhower thinks.

Fort Dodge, Iowa
October 5, 1952

The Republican Party is the party which makes even its young men seem old. The Democratic Party is the party which makes even its old men seem young.

Governor's Day
Illinois State Fair
Springfield, Illinois
August 14, 1952

I like a lot of Republicans, even some very new converts to that faith, whatever it is. Indeed there are some Republicans I would trust with anything—anything, that is, except public office.

Governor's Day
Illinois State Fair
Springfield, Illinois
August 14, 1952

When I came here today I met an old and dear friend, sprung from a staunch Republican family in Illinois, who has moved to Arizona and joined the Democratic Party! It reminded me of the story of the little boy who asked his father what a convert was, and the father—evidently a politically-minded father—said: "Well, son, if a Republican becomes a Democrat he is a convert." And what, asked

the boy, is a Democrat who becomes a Republican? With a scowl his father said: "Why, he's a traitor, of course."

Phoenix, Arizona
September 12, 1952

The Democratic Party is the people's party, not the labor party, not the farmers' party, not the employers' party —it is the party of no one because it is the party of everyone.

Acceptance speech
Democratic National Convention
Chicago, Illinois
July 26, 1952

We [the Democrats] have just been trying to give the people the right change, which seems to be a novel and appealing idea.

Governor's Day
Illinois State Fair
Springfield, Illinois
August 14, 1952

Noting that the platform from which General Eisenhower addressed an audience in Richmond, Virginia, had collapsed at the end of the General's speech, Stevenson said:

I'm glad the General wasn't hurt. But I wasn't surprised that it happened—I've been telling him for two months that nobody could stand on that platform.

Paducah, Kentucky
September 27, 1952

If the Republicans stop telling lies about us, we will stop telling the truth about them.

Bakersfield, California
September, 1952

The Democrats are denounced for not wanting changes and then they are denounced for a subversive desire to change everything. I'm beginning to wonder if the Republican campaign rests on the proposition that Democrats are social revolutionaries who want to keep things exactly as they are.

Colorado Volunteers for Stevenson Dinner
Denver, Colorado
September 5, 1952

I am no more in favor of socialism than anybody else, and I particularly dislike things that creep. But if I don't like what they call creeping socialism, there is something else I dislike just as much, and that is galloping reaction.

Los Angeles, California
September 11, 1952

In a speech before the Democratic National Committee's Southern Conference Dinner, closely following Senator Joseph McCarthy's attack on the Democratic Administration as "twenty years of treason," Mr. Stevenson said:

That such things are said under the official sponsorship of the Republican Party in celebration of the birthday of Abraham Lincoln adds desecration to defamation. This is the first time that politicians, Republicans at that, have sought to split the Union—in Lincoln's honor.

Miami Beach, Florida
March 7, 1954

I have finally figured out what the Republican orators mean by what they call "moderate progressivism." All they mean is: "Don't just do something. Stand there."

Hartford, Connecticut
February 25, 1956

Now I shall have to confess that the Republican Administration has performed a minor miracle. After twenty years of incessant damnation of the New Deal, they not only haven't repealed it but they have swallowed it . . . or at least most of it. And it looks as though they might be able to keep it down until at least after election.

Acceptance speech
Democratic National Convention
Chicago, Illinois
August 17, 1956

The Republicans have been in office for twenty months —or long enough to elect Maine's first Democratic governor in twenty years.

Democratic dinner
Indianapolis, Indiana
September 18, 1954

In an election year they pick a President and then for four years they pick on him.

To the State Committee of the Liberal Party
New York, New York
August 28, 1952

It seems to me very appropriate that the party with a heart should be having this great dinner here in New York

on St. Valentine's Day. I'm sure that we Democrats are in a mood to love everybody, and of course we'd be delighted if a few million more people would love us.

Jefferson Day Dinner
New York, New York
February 14, 1953

I am glad that I can spend a few minutes here with you this afternoon in Hamtramck. You know, one of the tests you have to pass in the freshman class in American Politics is to pronounce that name.

Hamtramck, Michigan
September 1, 1952

I shall not soon forget about the woman in the crowd in San Francisco who reached into the car to shake hands with me, and not long after discovered that she had lost her diamond ring. Nor will I forget the warm welcome I received on a whistle stop in Bethlehem and my thanks to "the people of Allentown." My only hope is that *they* forget it!

Major Campaign Speeches of Adlai E. Stevenson
Random House, 1953

Thousands wrote gracious, flattering letters, after the election, explaining why they did *not* vote for me. They seemed to feel they owed me an explanation. I was touched and flattered, but, I confess the thought occurred to me that a little "x" in the right place on the ballot would have been so much easier than a long, thoughtful letter.

Major Campaign Speeches of Adlai E. Stevenson
Random House, 1953

If you run for office and have a slightly unusual name, let me advise you either to change it before you start, or be prepared to take other people's word for it.

Major Campaign Speeches of Adlai E. Stevenson
Random House, 1953

Courage to do the right thing in public office is often at the price of the office.

Conversation with Arnold Michaelis
Libertyville, Illinois
June 19, 1956

Sheer physical exhaustion was for me a continuous and disquieting menace to equilibrium, judgment and creative concentration.

Major Campaign Speeches of Adlai E. Stevenson
Random House, 1953

I suppose we have contrived few more exacting ordeals than a Presidential campaign.

Major Campaign Speeches of Adlai E. Stevenson
Random House, 1953

Each of us thinks the other mature if he votes the same way for the same reason. And, because intellectual pride is here to stay, each of us is likely to feel that he understands things a little better than the next man.

Major Campaign Speeches of Adlai E. Stevenson
Random House, 1953

I have said what I meant and meant what I said. I have not done as well as I should like to have done, but I have done my best, frankly and forthrightly; no man can do more and you are entitled to no less.

Chicago, Illinois
November 3, 1952

Upon losing the 1952 Presidential election, he quipped:

Someone asked me, as I came in down on the street, how I felt. I was reminded of a story that a fellow townsman of ours used to tell—Abraham Lincoln. They asked him how he felt once after an unsuccessful election. He said he felt like a little boy who had stubbed his toe in the dark; that he was too old to cry, but it hurt too much to laugh.

Concession speech
Election night
November, 1952

Did I talk over the people's heads? No—and that's about the only aspect of the campaign I am sure of!

Major Campaign Speeches of Adlai E. Stevenson
Random House, 1953

Speaking to a television audience after his first unsuccessful Presidential campaign:

A funny thing happened to me on the way to the White House . . .

Washington, D.C.
December 13, 1952

Arriving late for a speech, Mr. Stevenson explained that he had been held up by a military parade and said:

Military heroes are always getting in my way.

Replying to the question whether he, as a boy, ever thought that he might end up running for President:

Yes, but I just dismissed it as a normal risk that any red-blooded American boy has to take.

The Presidency is an office that "converts vanity to prayer."

"Face the Nation" (CBS)
July 10, 1960

After declining to run a third time and upon being asked who he thought was the best man for the Presidency:

I think it's an office now which is so fated with the hopes, the fears of countless millions of people, not only in the United States but all over the world . . . that it's very hard for anyone to presume to say that he's the best fitted man for that office. I don't think anybody is wholly fitted for that office.

"Face the Nation" (CBS)
July 10, 1960

Discussing President Kennedy's appointment of several men from Mr. Stevenson's law firm in Chicago:

I regret that I have but one law firm to give to my country.

My opponents say that America cannot afford to be strong. I say that America cannot afford to be weak.

Louisville, Kentucky
September 27, 1952

[44]

There are rising voices here and abroad that forget that although America occasionally gags on a gnat, it also has some talent for swallowing tigers whole . . .

Columbia University Bicentennial Conference
New York, New York
June 5, 1954

There are no short cuts to national security. There are only short cuts to defeat.

Radio broadcast to the Armed Forces overseas
August 30, 1952

The only way you could cut tens of billions from your budget would be to disband our armies, renounce our friends abroad, quit buying airplanes and guns, cancel our present defense orders and, presumably, crawl into a cave to await destruction.

Indianapolis, Indiana
September 27, 1952

All the bushels of wheat and the nuclear reactors and dollars in creation will do us little good if they seem only to be the bait with which a rich but uncertain nation seeks to buy protection for itself. If our attitude is wrong, no amount of money can do the job; and if our attitude is right, less money will go further.

To the American Society of Newspaper Editors
Washington, D.C.
April 21, 1956

We need our Allies, as they need us. The fact that we have been in a position to contribute most to our collective defense in the way of arms and money does not entitle us to preach or threaten . . . we want no sullen obedience, but friendly co-operation . . . we want no satellites, we want companions in arms.

Jefferson Day Dinner
New York, New York
February 14, 1953

Replying to Secretary of State John Foster Dulles' announcement that the United States would retaliate with nuclear weapons in the event of a Communist attack:

It has been presented to us as a program of more for our money—national security in the large economy size package—"a bigger bang for a buck."

National Democratic Committee's Southern Conference
Miami Beach, Florida
March 7, 1954

It is odd that one of the keys to abundance should have been handed to civilization on a platter of destruction.

To the American Legion
Madison Square Garden
New York, New York
August 27, 1952

This is a new dimension in man's life and the life of society in civilization, because never before have we had this power of self-destruction as we have it now.

I hope that we can make nuclear energy man's servant and not man's destructive master. Clearly this must be the test . . . for which man's intelligence and the evolution of his thinking has been devised.

Conversation with Arnold Michaelis
Libertyville, Illinois
June 19, 1956

There is no evil in the atom; only in men's souls.

Hartford, Connecticut
September 18, 1952

A genuine partnership operates through consultation and persuasion. There is no room in it for the "Big Stick" or the ultimatum, be it the small or the medium size or even the large economy size. Ours must be the role of the good neighbor. The good partner, the good friend. Never, the big bully.

Jefferson Day Dinner
New York, New York
February 14, 1953

We will frighten no Russians by threatening our Allies.

Jefferson Day Dinner
New York, New York
February 14, 1953

Hunting scapegoats is not a foreign policy.

Founders Day
Northwestern University
Evanston, Illinois
January 28, 1951

Our mission is the prevention, not just the survival, of a major war . . . There are no Gibraltars, no fortresses impregnable to death or ideas any more.

Founders Day
Northwestern University
Evanston, Illinois
January 28, 1951

[48]

Science has destroyed any rational excuse for war between states.

UN Twentieth Anniversary
San Francisco, California
June 26, 1965

Science has given us the knowledge, and technology has given us the tools, and common sense has given us the wit to perceive that common interest impels us to common enterprise.

UN Twentieth Anniversary
San Francisco, California
June 26, 1965

The First World War was a shock, but not a lesson.

The New York Times Magazine
November 6, 1949

The enemy is not change but violence. To induce needed change without needless murder, what we require above all is a truce to terror. We need a moratorium—a breathing spell free from acts of international violence.

UN Twentieth Anniversary
San Francisco, California
June 26, 1965

The quest for peace and security is not a day's or a decade's work. For us it may be everlasting.

Godkin Lectures
Harvard University
March 15, 1954

[49]

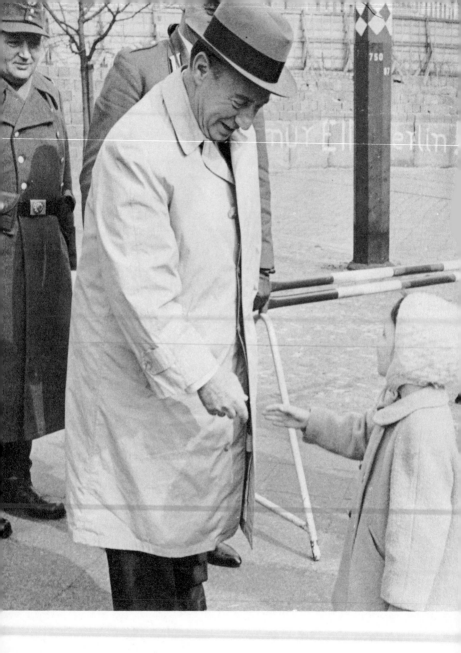

How elusive is peace—how durable is man's destructive drive—how various are the forms of his aggressions.

UN Twentieth Anniversary
San Francisco, California
June 26, 1965

World order will come not through the purity of the human heart nor the purge of the human soul, but will be wrought from a thousand common ventures that are at once possible and imperative.

UN Twentieth Anniversary
San Francisco, California
June 26, 1965

Retreat leads to retreat just as aggression leads to aggression in this still primitive international community.

Address to Harvard alumni
Cambridge, Massachusetts
June 17, 1965

Defeat begins in the heart . . . we must not allow the recklessness of despair to find any lodging in our hearts.

Hamtramck, Michigan
September 1, 1952

I pray that the imagination we unlock for defense and arms and outer space may be unlocked as well for grace and beauty in our daily lives. As an economy, we need it. As a society, we shall perish without it.

Tufts University
June 8, 1962

[52]

Only men who confuse themselves with God would dare to pretend in this anguished and bloody era that they know the exact road to the promised land.

To the State Committee of the Liberal Party
New York, New York
August 28, 1952

The will to peace cannot be legislated. It must be developed, and can only be developed by organized, patient effort. The laws and institutions of international co-operation have to evolve out of a combination of the common aspirations and experience of the peoples of the world.

London
1945

There is not a single dispute in this world—however sharply the issues may be drawn—which would not look different two decades from now, after time and change have done their erosive work on the sharpest corners of conflict.

UN Twentieth Anniversary
San Francisco, California
June 26, 1965

In our interdependent world there is no longer any line of demarcation between social and political problems. The solution of one depends on how well we understand the other and the extent to which we succeed in doing both.

Commencement address
Colby College
Waterville, Maine
June 7, 1964

In the bright glow of 1945 too many looked to the United Nations for the full and final answer to world peace. And in retrospect that day may seem to have opened with the hint of a false dawn.

UN Twentieth Anniversary
San Francisco, California
June 26, 1965

We are trying to construct a civilized world for the genus man . . . This aim may appear one of high generality. But so are such phrases as "the defense of national interests," or "lebensraum," or "the white man's burden," or any of the other catch phrases with which men have gone out with good conscience to plunder and maim their neighbors.

Conference on World Tensions
University of Chicago
May 12, 1960

The United Nations is of first interest above all to the weaker states since without it they have no ultimate protection against the force of more powerful and predatory governments.

New York, New York
March 2, 1961

Without it [the United Nations] we would have to try to create it. To create it now might even be impossible . . . witness all of these threats to international peace and security which in the nuclear age could rapidly escalate into a war which wouldn't kill millions but which would destroy everyone. This has to be prevented at all costs. It's for this

that the political activities of the UN exist . . . they have not accomplished everything but they have accomplished something.

"Issues and Answers" (ABC)
April 19, 1964

We shared an audacious dream—and launched a brave enterprise.

UN Twentieth Anniversary
San Francisco, California
June 26, 1965

If Communism is a problem for the United Nations, so is the United Nations a problem for Communism. The United Nations is a community of tolerance and a community of tolerance is a terrible frustration to the totalitarian mind.

United Nations
New York, New York
June 19, 1962

I tell you now that I will never fear to negotiate in good faith with the Soviet Union, for to close the door to the conference room is to open a door to war. Man's tragedy has all too often been that he has grown weary in the search for an honorable alternative to war, and, in desperate impatience, has turned to violence.

Hamtramck, Michigan
September 1, 1952

Democracy takes into account the factor to which Communism seems so invincibly obtuse: the unsearchable depths of the mind and spirit of man, who will forever thwart the attempts of dogma and ideology to predict him or to hem him in.

The New York Times Magazine
November 4, 1962

Communism knows no God, and cannot satisfy the hungry heart.

Major Campaign Speeches of Adlai E. Stevenson
Random House, 1953

The answer to Communism is, in the old-fashioned phrase, good works—good works inspired by love and dedicated to the whole man. The answer to the inhumanity of Communism is humane respect for the individual.

San Francisco, California
September 9, 1952

We shall never be able to cope with Communism unless we understand the emotional basis of its appeal.

San Francisco, California
September 9, 1952

Communism has already enveloped and enslaved many hapless millions through the world. It has drawn people to serve under false gods . . . and it has imbued them with the devil's own fury.

Radio broadcast to the Armed Forces overseas
August 30, 1952

There are laws of history more profound, more inescapable than the laws dreamed up by Marx and Lenin—

laws which belong not to class relationships or stages of economic development but to the nature and destiny of man himself. Among these laws is the certainty that war follows when new empires thrust into collapsing ruins of the old. Let there be no doubt about the alternatives. They are written unhappily in words of blood and flame on the walls of the world.

New York, New York
March 2, 1961

Communism has yet to be the popular choice of one single nation anywhere on the face of the globe. In the few places where it has extended its control, whether in Czechoslovakia, North Vietnam, or Cuba, it has been in the same classic role—as the scavenger of war and of ruined revolutions.

The New York Times Magazine
November 4, 1962

[Communism] organizes terror. It is without spiritual content or comfort. It provides no basic security. In the long run, it cannot cure the disease of this anxious age. But its short-term methods are grimly effective.

Communism is the corruption of a dream of justice.

Urbana, Illinois
1951

Dammit, Andrei [Gromyko], you fellows can't have everything!

While acting U.S. delegate to
the United Nations Preparatory Commission
London
October 24, 1945

We are suckers for good news, but we dare not be beguiled by a more conciliatory Soviet Union and by our strident, shallow voices who are its unwitting tools . . . The millennium has not arrived; sweetness and light is still an illusion; objectives have not changed in Moscow, only tactics.

United Nations Festival
Rantoul, Illinois
October 1, 1950

During the Security Council debates on the Cuba missile crisis in 1962, Soviet Ambassador Valerian Zorin accused the United States of worsening the situation by instituting a blockade of Cuba. This was Stevenson's reply:

To those who say that a limited quarantine was too much, in spite of the provocation and the danger, let me tell you a story, attributed to Abraham Lincoln, about the passer-by out in my part of the country who was charged by a farmer's ferocious boar. He picked up a pitchfork and met the boar head on. It died, and the irate farmer denounced him and asked him why he didn't use the blunt end of the pitchfork, and the man replied, "Why didn't the boar attack me with his blunt end?"

UN Security Council
New York, New York
October, 1962

Introducing President John F. Kennedy following the Cuban missile crisis:

And now it is my great privilege to introduce to you the author, the producer, the director, and the star of Mr.

Khrushchev's new hit play in Moscow, "A Funny Thing Happened to Me on My Way to Cuba."

Awards Dinner
Joseph P. Kennedy, Jr., Foundation
Washington, D.C.
December 7, 1962

A free society means a society based on free competition and there is no more important competition than competition in ideas, competition in opinion. This form of competition is essential to the preservation of a free press.

Portland Journal luncheon for Oregon newspapermen
Portland, Oregon
September 8, 1952

The rock bottom foundation of a free press is the integrity of the people who run it. Our press may make a million mistakes of judgment without doing itself permanent harm so long as its proprietors are steadfast in their adherence to truth.

Portland, Oregon
September 8, 1952

It's not honest convictions honestly stated that concern me. Rather it is the tendency of many papers, and I include columnists, commentators, analysts, feature writers, and so on, to argue editorially from the personal objective, rather than from the whole truth. As the old jury lawyer said: "And these, gentlemen, are the conclusions on which I base my facts."

Portland Journal luncheon for Oregon newspapermen
Portland, Oregon
September 8, 1952

[61]

Your typewriter is a public trust. The sound may be the most beautiful noise you know. But it has meaning and justification only if it is part of the gloriously discordant symphony of a free society.

Gridiron Dinner
December 12, 1960
Washington, D.C.

It would seem that the overwhelming majority of the press is . . . against Democrats. And it is against Democrats, so far as I can see, not after a sober and considered review of the alternatives, but automatically, as dogs are against cats. As soon as a newspaper—I speak of the great majority, not of the enlightened ten per cent—sees a Democratic candidate it is filled with an unconquerable yen to chase him up an alley.

Portland Journal luncheon for Oregon newspapermen
Portland, Oregon
September 8, 1952

I've been much interested in the continued debate that's been raging in the newspapers as to whether I was headed right, center, or left. I think it would have been rather more relevant had they asked: Is the man moving forward, backward, or is he grounded?

To the State Committee of the Liberal Party
New York, New York
August 28, 1952

I have always marveled at the ingenuity of certain members of the fourth estate in creating news. They even linked my name, some time ago, with Margaret Truman's,

romantically . . . but that was before we had met. And since she met me, nothing else has appeared.

Jefferson Day Dinner
New York, New York
February 14, 1953

I'm convinced that most of the press of this country follow Joseph Pulitzer's admonition: his remark that accuracy is to a newspaper what virtue is to a lady. Except, as someone pointed out, a newspaper can always print a retraction.

Awards Dinner
Joseph P. Kennedy, Jr., Foundation
Washington, D.C.
December 7, 1962

I seem to spend an awful lot of time reading about myself in papers and magazines these days. The awful thing is, I can't say I mind it much either.

Springfield, Illinois
1952

At a luncheon for newspaper editors and publishers:

I am convinced that nearly all [newspaper] publishers are doing their honest best, according to their lights—even if I must confess that sometimes their lights seem to me a little dim.

Portland, Oregon
September 8, 1952

Legality is not a synonym for morality.

Springfield, Illinois

I think it is just as important to recognize and support the good as to find and punish the bad.

Springfield, Illinois

We have not, we do not, and we will not condone, excuse, or explain away wrong-doing or moral obliquity in public office, whoever the guilty and whatever their station . . .. One corrupt official is one too many.

Democratic National Committee dinner
Chicago, Illinois
December 13, 1951

Military power without a moral base is always intolerable.

Springfield, Illinois

Let none of us, fighting man or civilian, ever forget that force without justice is tyranny . . . Let us never forget that justice without force is impotent, futile, and useless in the world we know.

United Nations Festival
Rantoul, Illinois
October 1, 1950

Law enforcement doesn't exist in a vacuum, and it can't be considered in isolation . . . You can't expect good government in other departments along with dishonest or ineffective law enforcement, and you can't have effective law enforcement without honest, efficient, responsible government all down the line.

To the American Bar Association
Washington, D.C.
September 19, 1950

[65]

On the subject of aid to education:

We cannot afford to be penny-wise and people-foolish.
Milwaukee, Wisconsin
September 28, 1956

The sources of information are the springs from which democracy drinks.

Cincinnati, Ohio
October 19, 1956

If I would guide you, I could not. What a man knows at fifty that he did not know at twenty is for the most part incommunicable.

The knowledge he has acquired with age is not the knowledge of formulas or forms of words, but of people, places, action—a knowledge not gained by words but by touch, sight, sound, victories, failures, sleeplessness, devotion, love . . . the human experiences and emotions of this earth and of one's self and of other men and perhaps, too, a little faith and a little reverence for the things you cannot see.

Commencement address
Princeton University
June 16, 1954

Following a visit in October, 1963, to Dallas, where he was greeted by a jeering crowd of far-right extremists:

A woman hit me on the head with a placard, and a man hit me on the cheek with a different weapon . . . I asked the angry police not to prefer charges against them,

not to punish them; after all, I didn't want them to go to jail—I thought it would be better if they went to school.

Los Angeles, California
October 24, 1963

Words calculated to catch everyone may catch no one.

Welcoming address
Democratic National Convention
Chicago, Illinois
July 21, 1952

Without fear we would never act in time to save ourselves, but I would warn with all of the certainty that I possess against permitting fear to seize our mind, to cloud our brain, and to paralyze our will.

Los Angeles, California
September 11, 1952

I am a great believer in national humility, modesty, self-examination and self-criticism, and I have preached these virtues vigorously, although, of course, I haven't practiced them very diligently.

Columbia University Bicentennial Conference
New York, New York
June 5, 1954

You can tell the size of a man by the size of the thing that makes him mad.

To the State Committee of the Liberal Party
New York, New York
August 28, 1952

All great students and practitioners of democracy have understood [the wisdom of humility]. Justice Oliver Wendell Holmes was once asked by what great principle his judicial opinions were guided, and he said: "I have spent seventy years finding out that I am not God."

The New York Times Magazine
November 4, 1962

Words are so easy, action is so difficult. To proclaim one's beliefs, to profess one's convictions is one thing; to enact them, to do them, to face the hard ugly realities . . . is quite another.

Conversation with Arnold Michaelis
Libertyville, Illinois
June 19, 1956

If what I've *said* falls short of what I *think*, well, ". . . a man's reach should exceed his grasp, or what's a heaven for?"

What I Think
By Adlai E. Stevenson
Harper and Row, 1955

Man does not live by words alone in spite of the fact that sometimes he has to eat them.

Gridiron Dinner
December 12, 1960
Washington, D.C.

Sometimes in the deafening clamor of political sales-manship, I've thought that the people might be better served

[69]

if a party purchased a half hour of radio and TV silence during which the audience would be asked to think quietly for themselves.

Major Campaign Speeches of Adlai E. Stevenson
Random House, 1953

You can't be contemptuous or tricky or condescending or secretive with the electorate. You've got to assume that the people are just as able to understand what's best . . . just as much as you do. If this weren't true, life wouldn't be worth living.

Joseph Alsop in the Saturday Evening Post
Quoting Adlai Stevenson
June 28, 1952

I sometimes marvel at the extraordinary docility with which Americans submit to speeches.

To the American Legion
Chicago, Illinois
September 11, 1950

When I was a boy I never had much sympathy for a holiday speaker. He was just a kind of interruption between the hot dogs; a fly in the lemonade.

Flint, Michigan
1952

Listening isn't easy. It isn't easy especially if you live in this extrovert world [of politics] that I've gotten into here in these recent years. But to really listen to someone you have to think of not only what he's saying but you also

[70]

have to understand what he means. And what he says and what he means, in view of the deficiencies and the inadequacies of self-expression, are not always the same thing.

Conversation with Arnold Michaelis
Libertyville, Illinois
June 19, 1956

I'm a strong believer in the right not to listen. And when you make as many speeches as I do, you soon become an authority on how boring they can be—especially to the fellow making them! But . . .

Milwaukee, Wisconsin
September 28, 1956

Mr. Stevenson's rule for speechwriting:

If you would make a speech or write one
Or get an artist to indite one,
Think not because 'tis understood
By men of sense, 'tis therefore good.
Make it so clear and simply planned
No blockhead can misunderstand.

The New York Herald Tribune
October, 1960

There is a spiritual hunger in the world today . . . and it cannot be satisfied by better cars on longer credit terms.

Acceptance speech
Democratic National Convention
Chicago, Illinois
August 17, 1956

In quiet places, reason abounds . . . in quiet people there is vision and purpose . . . many things are revealed to the humble that are hidden from the great.

A wise man does not try to hurry history.

San Francisco, California
September 9, 1952

I don't like doles. I don't like subsidies. I don't like any interference with free markets, free men, and free enterprise. I like freedom to succeed or to fail. But I also know that there can be no real freedom without economic justice, social justice, equality of opportunity, and a fair chance for every individual to make the most of himself.

New York Herald Tribune Forum
New York, New York
October 24, 1949

Greatness cannot be measured alone by the conventional yardsticks of resources, know-how, and production.

Major Campaign Speeches of Adlai E. Stevenson
Random House, 1953

In our own prosperous days a new possibility has arisen: that the many can smugly overlook the squalor and misery of the few, and tolerate in the midst of unparalleled plenty, ugly slums, rural destitution, and second-class citizenship.

"America's Image of Greatness"
Life magazine
May 30, 1960

The goal of life is more than material advance; it is now, and through all eternity, the triumph of spirit over matter, of love and liberty over force and violence.

Major Campaign Speeches of Adlai E. Stevenson
Random House, 1953

We are struggling to *meet* grievous assault by better satisfying the basic material needs of man. But we shall *master* the assault only by better satisfying the basic spiritual needs of man. These are hungers too.

Major Campaign Speeches of Adlai E. Stevenson
Random House, 1953

The contrast between private opulence and public squalor on most of our panorama is now too obvious to be denied. Yet we still spend per capita almost as much on advertising to multiply the private wants of our people as we do on education to enable them to seek a fuller, wiser, and more satisfying civic existence.

"America's Image of Greatness"
Life magazine
May 30, 1960

If I were asked to choose a single principle which underlines more than any other the difference between the Communist and the free philosophy, it would be this issue of criticism which we in the West not only tolerate, but esteem.

What I Think
By Adlai E. Stevenson
Harper and Row, 1955

The face which we present to the world, especially through our mass circulation media, is the face of the individual or the family as a high consumption unit with minimal social responsibilities—father happily drinking his favorite beer, mother dreamily fondling soft garments newly rinsed in a wonderful new detergent, the children gaily calling from the barbecue pit for a famous sauce for their steak.

"America's Image of Greatness"
Life magazine
May 30, 1960

With the supermarket as our temple and the singing commercial as our litany, are we likely to fire the world with an irresistible vision of America's exalted purposes and inspiring way of life?

"America's Image of Greatness"
Life magazine
May 30, 1960

Criticism, in its fairest and most honest form, is the attempt to test whether what is, might not be better.

What I Think
By Adlai E. Stevenson
Harper and Row, 1955

Criticism, not as an instrument of inquiry and reform, but as an instrument of power, quickly degenerates into the techniques of deceit and smear.

What I Think
By Adlai E. Stevenson
Harper and Row, 1955

Timing—timing with respect to change—is as important as change itself.

Colorado Volunteers for Stevenson Dinner
Denver, Colorado
September 5, 1952

Let me say at the outset, that if anyone doesn't hate high taxes . . . well, he just hasn't paid his taxes.

Democratic State Convention
Green Bay, Wisconsin
October 7, 1955

Technology, while adding daily to our physical ease, throws daily another loop of fine wire around our souls.

"My Faith in Democratic Capitalism"
Fortune magazine
October, 1955

Laughter is shared by equals. It cannot be bestowed with condescension.

Foreword to RCA album
"The Wit of JFK"

From a message to the Illinois State Senate explaining his veto of a bill intended to restrict the freedom of cats:

I cannot agree that it should be the declared public policy of Illinois that a cat visiting a neighbor's yard or crossing the highway is a public nuisance. It is in the nature of cats to do a certain amount of unescorted roaming . . . to escort a cat abroad on a leash is against the nature of the owner. Moreover, cats perform useful service, particularly in the rural areas. The problem of the cat vs. the bird is as old as time. If we attempt to resolve it by legislation, who knows but what we may be called upon to take sides as well in the age-old problems of dog vs. cat, bird vs. bird, or even bird vs. worm. In my opinion, the State of Illinois and its local governing bodies already have enough to do without trying to control feline delinquency.

Springfield, Illinois
April 23, 1949

It's the hardest thing in the world. I can think, personally, of no worse punishment than somehow to be confronted with one's own cowardice.

Conversation with Arnold Michaelis
Libertyville, Illinois
June 19, 1956

Solemnity in politicians is not only tiresome, but may even mask those twin sins, self-righteousness and intolerance for the opinions of others.

Foreword to RCA album
"The Wit of JFK"

If I couldn't laugh, I couldn't live—especially in politics.

Foreword to RCA album
"The Wit of JFK"

Stevenson's favorite prayer . . . from St. Francis of Assisi:

Let me be an instrument of thy peace.

Adlai Stevenson's paternal grandmother's family founded the Bloomington *(Illinois)* Daily Pantagraph. *Early in his career, Stevenson worked on the paper as a reporter (among other things he did a series of articles on the Scopes trial in Tennessee), as a foreign correspondent for Hearst's International News Service, and as an editor. Later in his life, he was to rank journalism with politics as among the noblest of professions. Indeed, according to one story, he nearly stayed in that profession.*

While Stevenson was an undergraduate at Princeton, he was approached by two newly minted Yale graduates, by the names of Hadden and Luce. They were, the two announced, about to embark on a new project, a news magazine, and did Stevenson want to invest, or possibly even join them in the venture. Stevenson declined because he had just put his money into a car invention. It's unclear what happened to the car invention, but history records that Time *magazine went on to make a fairly respectable showing.*

One of his first assignments as a cub reporter with the Bloomington Daily Pantagraph *was to help another reporter cover a watermelon eating contest. The* Pantagraph *points out that Stevenson entered the contest himself ". . . and was a definite contender until the reporter hauled him away."*

———◆———

His great-grandfather, Jesse Fell, was a close friend of Abraham Lincoln; indeed he was the first man to propose that Lincoln run for the Presidency. His grandfather, Adlai E. Stevenson, was elected Vice-President of the United

States on the Grover Cleveland ticket. His father was Secretary of State for Illinois.

"I," Stevenson once said, "had a bad case of hereditary politics."

———◆———

During the period that he was Governor of Illinois, it was Stevenson's custom to hold an annual Christmas party for his children and their friends. Most of the boys were usually put up at a downtown hotel, while the girls were invited to stay at the Governor's Mansion. One year, however, a small group of the boys was given a back room of the mansion. It was quickly dubbed "the casino." For the Stevenson youngsters had installed a toy roulette wheel there and occasionally played for pennies.

Coincidentally, at this time, Governor Stevenson had been waging a state-wide war against gambling. Even so, he didn't say anything when, one afternoon, he went back to "the casino" to get the boys to join the girls out front. That he noticed the presence of that toy roulette wheel there is little doubt, because a short while later, guests were treated to the specter of a room in the Governor's Mansion being "raided" by a pair of burly state troopers.

It is said that the Stevenson children learned a valuable lesson and that the governor laughed for days.

———◆———

In retrospect, the Stevenson camp of 1956 reads like an honor roll of success stories. John Kenneth Galbraith, who was later to become U.S. Ambassador to India; Arthur

Schlesinger, Jr., who rose to prominence as a member of the inner circle of Kennedy advisers; Willard Wirtz, who was to be named Secretary of Labor; and Newton Minnow, who became perhaps the best-known and most highly respected chairman of the Federal Communications Commission. There was another man who accompanied the candidate. He took extensive notes, asked a lot of questions; but it was a little difficult to pin down precisely what he was doing in the campaign. Four years later, it was very clear. Robert Kennedy had been a most attentive observer.

———————◆———————

In the Stevenson camp, they were calling the campaign of 1956 the "prop-stop" campaign. For the first time in the history of American politics planes were supplanting the more traditional "whistle stop."

On this particular occasion, however, the candidate was traveling by train. A warm admirer of President Woodrow Wilson, Stevenson was using a caboose-like car that had carried Wilson nearly five decades earlier.

It was late in the campaign. They were in Michigan. Stevenson was about to make his first speech of the day. His train had pulled into a siding near a sprawling factory. The candidate was introduced, walked up to the microphone stand, and tried to adjust the mike to his own level. It stuck. As Stevenson strained, an aide jumped to his side and loosened the grip-tightener on the microphone pole. Stevenson quipped: "I guess I didn't have my Wheaties this morning." To everyone's surprise, the crowd groaned, hissed, and booed. The candidate looked up. There on the side of the factory was the legend: "KELLOGG'S of Battle Creek."

[82]

In 1956 the electoral vote that proclaimed Eisenhower the winner over Stevenson was a thundering 457–74. Stevenson was asked for his reaction. Once again, he drew on Lincoln: "Disappointed, yes; bruised, no." But when he was asked whether he might ever head his party's ticket again, he shuddered, and said, "Perish forbid!"

◆

To the dismay of his advisers, Stevenson refused during most of the 1956 campaign to make any personal attacks on his opponent, Dwight Eisenhower, a refusal that would be somewhat unusual in any election. By most campaign standards, the President also was mild in his attacks; but he had consistently been needling Stevenson on the quips that he interjected into his speeches with such abandon. Eisenhower called Stevenson the candidate who would tell jokes rather than discuss issues.

Finally, Stevenson struck back: "I refuse," he said, "to conform to the Republican law of gravity."

◆

By and large, Stevenson got little support from the newspaper and magazine publishers of America; but among the working press, it was a different story. He was an immensely popular candidate with reporters and photographers.

On one occasion, Stevenson was walking into the Kansas City Opera House. In front of the candidate three news photographers backed their way into the hall, snapping pictures as they moved along. Amid the confusion, Stevenson

tripped on a rug and would have fallen, had not two of the photographers dropped their cameras and caught him. To the professional news photographers—each a charter member in the "shoot first, help later school"—only the closest family intimate merits this kind of consideration. As the caravan resumed its progress, one of the photographers made it clear that this courtesy would probably not have been extended to Stevenson's opponent, for he was heard to say ruefully:". . . if that'd only been Eisenhower, we'd've had a Pulitzer."

The hole-in-the-shoe was no incident of indifference to clothing. Adlai Stevenson had a "British-squirelike" devotion to favorite pieces of apparel. He would wear them, literally, until they fell apart at the seams. His daughter-in-law, Nancy, recalls the time that Stevenson was stopped by a man in downtown Chicago, who pointed out, "Governor, your lining is hanging down." Stevenson reached into a pocket, pulled out a paper clip, and repaired the offending jacket. Nancy Stevenson insists the Governor of Illinois had been walking around that way for a week.

When Adlai Stevenson did not choose to answer a question, he could be as skillfully evasive as any other politician. A few days before the 1960 Democratic Convention in Los Angeles, reporters attempted to get the now twice-defeated Presidential candidate to state his choice for the party's

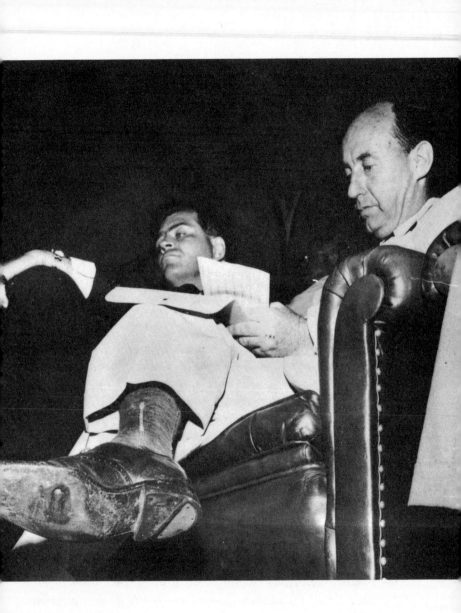

new standard bearer, the front-runners in the race being Lyndon B. Johnson and the youthful John F. Kennedy.

Reporter: Governor, would you share Senator Johnson's view that the times require a man who has a shot of gray in his hair and therefore Senator Kennedy is too young for the nomination?
Stevenson: It's awfully hard for a man in my condition to talk about hair. I'm at somewhat of a disadvantage, as you can see.

"Face the Nation" (CBS)
July 10, 1960

———◆———

Even late in life, burdened as he was by the complex and debilitating office of Ambassador to the United Nations, Adlai Stevenson found time for the thoughtfulness that characterized his entire demeanor.

In 1963, having learned that the eleven-year-old son of an information officer at the UN was ill of leukemia, Stevenson interrupted a busy workday, went to the boy's hospital room, chatted with him for about fifteen or twenty minutes, and then left. Stevenson knew the boy's father only casually.

———◆———

"I think," Adlai Stevenson's son, Borden, once said of his father, "that his attitude toward clothes is a manifestation of his personality. Dad hates anything he thinks is phony or pretentious."

Borden Stevenson went on to illustrate his father's atti-

tude toward clothes by recalling the time the elder Steven-
son had sent him into town to take an old suit to the tailor.
"Unless I'm mistaken," Borden quotes the old tailor as say-
ing, "unless I'm mistaken, and I doubt that, this is the same
suit I worked on for your father fifteen years ago."

———◆———

A man of immense compassion, Stevenson's favorite kind
of story tended to center on humor of which he was the
butt.

　He recalled a formal dinner in Jamaica back in 1955.
Princess Margaret of Great Britain was the guest of honor;
Stevenson was seated at her left. A spirited conversation-
alist, Stevenson was devoting his full attention to Her Royal
Highness, when he noticed that some gravy had spilled on
his hand. Without interrupting the flow of talk, Governor
Stevenson reached under the table for his napkin and began
wiping off the gravy. The Princess, who also boasts a well-
developed sense of humor, transfixed her dinner partner
with an icy stare and said: "Governor Stevenson, will you
kindly remove your filthy hand from my scarf?"

　The Governor noted later that a missed napkin nearly
ruptured Anglo-American relations.

———◆———

Stevenson used to love to tell this story about himself after
he became a world figure:

I had been away from my home town of Bloomington
a number of years and was asked to return to give a speech.

I had not expected a brass band, but I was a little surprised to find no welcoming committee. So I picked up my bag and as I passed Abe, an old baggageman who had known me since I was a boy, he raised his head and said, "Hello, Ad . . . been away?"

———◆———

Rotarians, on one occasion, experienced some difficulty in obtaining Stevenson as a speaker at their national convention. But they did finally succeed, and he referred to their difficulty:

I'm reminded of the preacher who told me he was much concerned about the reputation of a certain woman in his congregation, and he said to her one Sunday after the service, "Madam, I prayed for you last night for three hours." And she said, "Well, Reverend, you needn't have gone to all that trouble. If you'd have just telephoned, I'd have come right over."

Rotary International
Atlantic City, New Jersey
June 1, 1965

We, the human race, are fellow travelers on a tiny spaceship spinning through infinite space. We can wreck our ship, we can blow the human experiment into nothingness; and by every analogy of practical life, a quarrelsome ship's company and many hands on the steering gear is a good recipe for disaster.

United Nations
New York, New York
January 26, 1965

Oh, what I would really like is to just sit in the shade with a glass of wine in my hand and watch the dancers.
Conversation with CBS Correspondent Eric Sevareid
London, England
July 13, 1965

THE COMPILERS AND THEIR BOOK

EDWARD HANNA *is currently a producer for ABC Radio News, where he has worked for the past three years, first as a staff writer, later as correspondent. In 1963 he was voted "Radio Writer of the Year" in a nationwide poll of radio-TV critics and has received several other awards for his work in the news documentary field.*

HENRY HICKS *is producer of* ABC Reports. *Prior to this assignment he was a radio and television writer for ABC News and producer of a number of documentary shows. Earlier he was a reporter for United Press International and in 1962 was a Ford Foundation Fellow in International Reporting at Columbia University's Graduate School of Journalism.*

TED KOPPEL *is a graduate of Syracuse (B.S.) and Stanford (M.A.) Universities. A correspondent for the ABC Radio Network, he has written and narrated a number of documentaries, among them, "D-Day: The First 24 Hours," which was selected in a nationwide poll of radio-TV critics as one of the three best radio documentaries of 1964.*

THE WIT AND WISDOM OF ADLAI STEVENSON *(Hawthorn, 1965) was set in type by the Pyramid Composition Co., Inc., New York City. It was printed by Mahony & Roese, Inc., New York City, and bound by The Montauk Book Manufacturing Co., Inc., New York City. The text type is Times Roman, a type face originally designed for the London Times.*

A HAWTHORN BOOK